Wonderfully Made You

Deann Shaver Leisch

WestBow Press books may be ordered through booksellers or by contacting:

WestBow Press
A Division of Thomas Nelson & Zondervan
1663 Liberty Drive
Bloomington, IN 47403
www.westbowpress.com
844-714-3454

All Scripture quotations are taken from The Holy Bible, New International Version®, NIV® Copyright
© 1973, 1978, 1984, 2011 by Biblica, Inc.® Used by permission. All rights reserved worldwide.

ISBN: 978-1-6642-1810-9 (sc)
ISBN: 978-1-6642-1811-6 (e)

Library of Congress Control Number: 2020925919

Print information available on the last page.

WestBow Press rev. date: 11/17/2021

WESTBOW
P R E S S®
A DIVISION OF THOMAS NELSON
& ZONDERVAN

For my wonderful blessings,
Jarrod, Blaire, Camille, and Luke.
I'm so thankful God made you!

Everybody is different ...
How very unique are we!
Think if everyone were the same.
How boring would that be?

Short and stout or lean and tall,
Everyone is special, and Jesus loves us all!

Whatever your shape, whatever your size,
Remember God made you, and you are a prize!

"I praise you because I am fearfully and wonderfully made."
—Psalm 139:14

Whether you have straight hair, curly hair,
Brown, black, blonde, or red,
Be thankful for the hair that God put on your head!

"And even the very hairs of your head are all numbered."
—Matthew 10:30

Some people's noses are pointy and long,
While others are round and short.
Some noses are freckled,
And some like to snort.

Without your nose,
You could not smell
Chocolate chip cookies or a sweet red rose!

"...and walk in the way of love, just as Christ
loved us and gave Himself up for us as a
fragrant offering and sacrifice to God."
—Ephesians 5:2

Your eyes may be small or big and round.
What would you miss without them?
Well, just look around!

Without your eyes, you could not see
The sunshine, pretty flowers, or a big oak tree.
Thank God for your eyes and look about!
You'll see your family, your friends,
and even your dog, Scout!

"The eye is the lamp of the body. If your eyes are
good, your whole body will be full of light."
—Matthew 6:22

Listen! Do you hear those sounds?
Bells ringing, children singing,
Hands clapping, family laughing!

God blessed us with ears so that we could hear
"Good morning," "Good night," "I love
you," and "Sleep tight!"

"Ears that hear and eyes that see—
the Lord has made them both."
—Proverbs 20:12

Big teeth, tiny teeth
Narrow grin or wide,
Thin lips or full lips
Your smile you should never hide!

The Lord gave us a mouth to speak, sing, and smile.
To scream, tell stories, and giggle with friends for a while.

He also gave us mouths to be able to eat.
We get to enjoy fruit, ice cream, and all kinds of treats!

"His praise will always be on my lips."
—Psalm 34:1

Use your mouth the way God wants you to.
Be kind, encouraging, respectful, and true.

Always be careful not to hurt others with what you say.
Do not lie, do not be rude,
But instead use your mouth to pray!

"May the words of my mouth and the meditation
of my heart be pleasing in your sight."
—Psalm 19:14

Each of us are different in so many ways,
How we look, sound, think, and even how we get around.
Some people use their legs to move,
while others go in chairs.
No matter if you walk, jump, or roll,
God made you, and He cares!

"Cast all your anxiety on Him because He cares for you."
—1 Peter 5:7

What's most important in this world?
Is it what you have, what you look like,
or the color of your skin?
Of course not! What really matters is what lies within.

"Man looks at the outward appearance,
but the Lord looks at your heart."
—1 Samuel 16:7

God cares for you and loves you so.
He made you unlike anyone else and wants you to know
You are special, you are beautiful, and you are one of a kind.
You were created for a purpose and made by His design!

"For we are God's workmanship, created in
Christ Jesus to do good works, which God
prepared in advance for us to do."
—Ephesians 2:10

Printed in the United States
by Baker & Taylor Publisher Services